MUMBLING FOOL
An American President
by Sean Seville

The Pisser Presidential Trilogy

Part I Our First Orange President

Part II Mumbling Fool: An American President

Part III Cackling In The White House

Table of Contents

Career Politician

The sound of loud continuous squeaking came from within the Oval Office. This unnerving racket could be heard from the White House corridors. Now in his early eighties Bo Triden is the oldest sitting president in U.S. history. He was having too much fun.

Spinning round and round. Over and over again he persisted. Bo remained firmly affixed to the swivel chair that was positioned behind his desk. A little merry-go-round to enjoy, and Triden was the only man in possession of an e - ticket for this ride. Suddenly it happened, the chair spun out of control, hurling the president straight to the floor.

With his seat now overturned, Bo laid in agony while clutching his leg.

"Owwwie, my knee!" Bo exclaimed.

Several secret service men came crashing into the Oval Office, rushing to the aid of Mr. Triden. They helped him back onto his feet. Then the chair was put back in place.

All of the White House staff were aware that Bo was misbehaving and back to his old antics again. Playing during recess when he should've been working on the national budget in order to avoid a government shutdown. This sedulous civil servant has served in politics for over fifty years. His hard work and dedication has not gone unnoticed by the masses. Sacrifices were made to ensure a thriving future for our youth.

There isn't anything that can be used to tarnish or diminish this crusader's impeccable accomplishments, even those achieved before becoming commander in chief. With such a stellar record Triden can hold his head high.

Fighting for the American people and helping to enhance this country to a point where everyone flourishes. This is exactly what this man strives for.

I wish all of this were true.

Perhaps in the farthest regions of the Multiverse it is. However, in this dimension that fantasy is not remotely set in reality. What is factual is that Bo Triden's allegiance is not to the American people, but to the lobbyists and corporate donors. He must appease them at all costs if he is to remain in power and keep the money rolling in. These days it's not quite business as usual.

The president is mounted on a slippery slope of cognitive decline. It only seems to worsen with each passing day. All of the worst traits of this commander in chief have been coming forth at the most sporadic and inopportune times. His dementia is here to stay. Therefore, the baffling remarks, confusion, and utter obliviousness will continue in stride.

For this is the presidency of Bo Annette Triden.

In The Oval Office Attending To Important Matters.

Enter: Camille

It was the early 1970s. Six months had passed since Bo's wife died in a tragic car accident while attempting to accelerate and pass an incoming train. He car got stuck on the railroad track. The locomotive hit the automobile and was obliterated along with Bo's wife. The news dealt Bo a devastating hit (But not as hard as the one to his wife).

For a while it seemed that Triden wouldn't be able to fully recover and function. To know that he could never hold his beloved wife in his arms ever again was a catastrophic feeling.

After six months of mourning Bo suddenly had an epiphany. "Oh well, life goes on. And these wild oats aren't going to sow themselves," Triden thought.

It wasn't long before Bo began to scour the local high schools. Due to the legal ramifications of this type of search he decided soon after that a change of venue was necessary. College campuses became his new hunting ground. He eventually met Camille Miller. She was a senior student that took her education very seriously.

Bo did a fantastic job of dialing back his creepiness, despite it leaking and oozing out with ease. It was similar to a tire with a minute puncture. Sooner or later you're guaranteed to get a flat. At the time, Triden was a senator with two young sons. Camille didn't mind and she was rather understanding.

Accepting people for who they are and their circumstances is something that Camille never hesitated in doing. Camille thought Bo was a little odd at first but she eventually warmed up to his quirkiness. Triden courted Camille for two years, during which he proposed marriage repeatedly. To a certain degree Camille loved Bo.

Finally, she accepted his proposal just to shut him up.

At the time when this occurred Bo stopped kneeling and smiled.

"It seems that the fourteenth time's a charm," he said.

The couple became wedlocked inside of a chapel located in New York City. Hawaii was the destination for the honeymoon.

"Guess what, Bo? I purchased two more tickets so Moe and Lambert can accompany us. Isn't that exciting news?" Camille asked.

A frown quickly spread across Bo's face. "My two sons?" Bo asked. "What in the hell did you do that for? We're going on our honeymoon not a family vacation. I'm trying to get you in the butt while staying at an extravagant hotel and you fucked that up," Bo said.

Camille wagged her finger at Bo. "Listen we are all one big happy family now and that's the way it is. Where we go, they go," Camille said.

Bo grimaced due to being extremely displeased with current events.

"Damn it, Camille. You suck," Bo said.

The honeymoon did transpire just as Camille had planned. After the marriage had taken place and time marched forward, the couple welcomed a newborn baby girl to the family. They named her Allison. One more member of this budding brood.

One Sided Negotiations

During the mid 1990s the Mayor of San Francisco, Philly White had a late night rendezvous with an accomplished prosecutor who also happened to be his ex- girlfriend. Her name was Jacqueline Barris. This woman has a degree in political science, economics, and of course, law. Philly and Jacqueline dated for over a year and a half. It was during this juncture that Jacqueline had been appointed to several different divisions as overseer of both unemployment insurance and medical boards. Having friends in high places can certainly work to one's advantage. Barris considered herself intelligent and ambitious, also adamant about proving all of her detractors wrong. Philly was thirty years her senior but he simply didn't care. It was fun while it lasted.

White was an avaricious man. He always acquired what he wanted but it was never enough. The relationship was over but not Jacqueline's "good deeds". If Barris' career were to reach new heights she would have to continue doing the mayor's bidding. Philly informed Jacqueline of a terrific job opportunity.

It could possibly lead to an astounding career. The election for a new district attorney would soon be upon us, and Mayor White didn't hesitate in offering his endorsement to Jacqueline. Barris couldn't be happier at the prospect of becoming district attorney. Her career was on a completely different trajectory now.

She wouldn't allow anyone to stand in her way. Barris had come too far to turn back. The moon in the sky was finally within reach. Stars are now aligned with the Heavens above.

Justice for all...

Philly tapped Jacqueline on the shoulder, then he handed her a couple of small items.

"What are these?" She asked.

Mayor White had a huge grin on his face. "Knee pads," he replied. "There's one more job that I need you to do."

Truce

The time had come for a new election. Incumbent President, Ronald T. Dump was set to run against Bo Triden. By this time, Bo had fifty years of experience as a civil servant. He also served as former vice president to Harmack Labamba. The country was engulfed in utter chaos.

Change had become a desperate necessity, although he would need to choose a running mate. After conferring with his staff it was decided that the best option was to choose a woman of color. This turns the chosen running mate into a mere D.E.I. hire. Never- the- less, after careful consideration Bo would go with Jacqueline Barris. Truth be told, Triden was less than enthusiastic about this decision.

During the Democratic debates Barris accused Triden of being racist, doing everything in his power to make integration in schools illegal. He partnered with segregationists in an attempt to forge legislation that would make busing illegal. Triden remained angry about that debate.

"How dare she drudge up the truth?" He asked himself.

Despite all of this, Bo swallowed his pride and made the announcement. California Senator, Jacqueline Barris was ecstatic when she received the phone call from Triden. She knew that they had to put aside their differences, because they had to win this election... and that they did. The country would soon be privy to a whole new level of embarrassment. If former President Dump had become an international joke, welcome to the punchline.

Do you think that you can just pick
up a coconut that fell out of a tree?
Add Pineapple juice and cream.
Mix it all up in a blender.
Now that's how you make a Proper

Pinacolada!
Don't forget to serve with ice

Ha, ha, ha, ha!

I'm Jacqueline Barris
and I approved this Message.

19

Playdate

The news had gone viral and could be seen of an abundance of televised news outlets. Triden was at it again. Some of the oddest behavior ever exhibited publicly by a sitting president. Bo had fetishes that were down right uncanny. Sniffing the hair of women and young girls alike, giving unwanted shoulder massages, and whispering "sweet nothings" into the ear of a twelve year old.

Let us not forget Bo's new proposals in a misguided attempt to acquire the black vote for Triden's party during the midterm elections:

He offered forth new legislation in which the prices of all chicken products would be greatly reduced by twenty percent.

It would become illegal for an employer to fire you if you're less than thirty minutes late to work.

As a form of slavery reparations, every black person born in America is entitled to free watermelon for the rest of their lives, with or without seeds.

Let's just say that this did not go over well. Today Mr. Triden has become smitten with someone that he met during a political rally. Bo has been married to Camille for over forty years but he couldn't care less. The senile old fool has been bitten by the love bug, and he was ready to profess his feelings.

A few secret service men escorted the president to all of his required destinations. First he was taken by car, incognito, to a perfume shop to pick up one of the most popular fragrances.

Purchasing two dozen roses was a given. Bo made his assistant order two tickets for the opera, and then purchase the sexiest piece of lingerie he could find.

After making another stop at a nearby establishment, Bo was prepared to present himself to that "special someone" that had taken hold of his heart. The secret service men stood on stand by as Triden entered an apartment building. His assistant, Bob followed suit.

Fortunately, the door was unlocked. They took the elevator up to the fourth floor. They were looking for apartment 416. A couple of minutes after vacating the elevator the two men quickly found the place. Bo nervously but vehemently knocked on the door. It opened and a man named Alfredo appeared before Bo.

Once he was recognized, the president and his assistant were invited into the man's humble abode. Now in the living room, Bob stood there with his arms full of gifts, as Triden told Alfredo that he wanted to see his daughter. Alfredo found this request peculiar but he played along. His daughter emerged from her bedroom wearing the prettiest pink frock. Bo didn't waste a moment of his time. He started expressing his love and how much he yearned for her.

He gave her the roses, jewelry, perfume, and lingerie. Bob shook his head in disbelief. The last store that they stopped at happened to be a toy store where Bo purchased a Teddy Bear. The mouth of Emelia's father was wide open. He was completely awestricken.

Bob told the president that it was time to go. Triden refused to leave. His desire was to stay with Emelia forever and ever.

Bo didn't see anything wrong with this sentiment. He felt that Emelia was a very mature 19 year old woman. Bob told the president once again that they had to leave.

Then Triden told Bob how he felt about the little lady. His assistant shook his head once more.

"Sir, look again. That's not a 19 year old woman. She's an eight year old girl," Bob said.

Bo blinked several times then rubbed his eyes before focusing. Finally for the first time, he laid eyes on the 8 year old and saw her for what she truly is.

"Oh shit," Bo said.

Subsequently he ran with the speed of a 20 year old. Then he jumped before diving straight through the window pane. Bob hurried over to the window after he tip toed around broken glass that covered an enormous portion of the floor. He looked down and saw the president running across the street. The secret service men were in the car chasing after Triden.

Bo was currently operating in "spry mode". Bob apologized to both Alfredo and his daughter before calling a cab for himself. The assistant had every intention of meeting the president back at the White House. An ordeal of this magnitude is completely unnecessary, but not uncommon with this commander in chief.

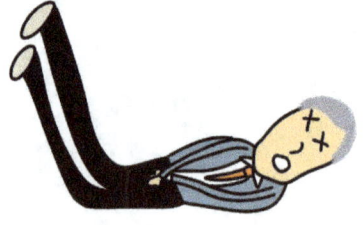

The Passage Of Time 2

Madam Vice President stood before the podium. As always she was nervous. Since the day Jacqueline was sworn into office she hadn't been the same. What happened to her intellect and wit ? Her college degrees and experience in government seemed to be moot.

Now she struggled to string a single sentence together. Absolutely clueless in her own intent. There was something growing inside of Jacqueline that laid dormant for so long. It had now awakened and it's making its way to the surface. Currently in the heart of Louisiana, Barris has returned in order to inspire hope, convey vital information regarding the president's agenda, and give encouragement to the American people. The vice president gave a speech here before that was met with monumental criticism.

Jacqueline returned here to rein in her constituents along with their respect. Barris cleared her throat. Then she began to speak with certainty and determination.

"Hello everyone, wakey, wakey, orgasm fakey. Ha, ha, ha, ha, ha, ha. Please have a seat. Take a load off," Jacqueline said.

Most of the spectators sat down in the chairs that were provided.

Barris continued on, "People live here like everybody else inside of a clock. This proverbial clock represents the passage of time," she said.

One of the spectators whispered to a friend that was standing next to him.

"Oh Hell, here we go again," he said. The friend sighed before giving a smirk.

Jacqueline continued, "A clock has numbers all around it. There are also hands. These represent the passage of time. If we wind the hands counterclockwise, we're traveling back in time. This is not our goal so we must get back to the future.

Ergo, the passage of time. Do we do this in a speed boat? How about a submarine? They no longer manufacture Deloreans. So how do we accomplish this daunting task?

A brand new vessel must be utilized. I propose that we use a toilet with seat heating capabilities. Scientists can begin work on this immediately. After flushing three times the mechanism will open a portal, granting us access to the space-time continuum. Of course you may stay seated on this ride at all times. Ha, ha, ha, ha, ha, ha, ha, ha.

Once our scientific team has created a toilet that can flush faster than the speed of light, time travel will be possible. In order to achieve this goal government funding will be a necessary. We might have to raise property taxes and gas prices all across the country but in the end the American people will stand tall before they sit down... on the commode. Speaking of the passage of time, there was a little passage of gas.

Ha, ha, ha, ha. Who did it?" Jacqueline asked.

All of the spectators and news reporters chattered among themselves. A reporter named Dan Y. Rivers stood up from his chair.

"Whoever smelt it, dealt it," he said.

Jacqueline frowned as many of the spectators laughed in glee. Another reporter named Stacy Grandholm stood to her feet before speaking.

"Madam Vice President, Why do you always laugh at such stupid shit?" She asked.

Many more of the vice president's constituents engaged in thunderous laughter. Some of them began to heckle Barris. A large urine stain appeared in the front of Barris' pants. This action caused an increase of laughter from these onlookers. Reporters zoomed in with their video cameras.

Urine trickled down Barris' pants and dripped out onto one of her shoes. A silent chuckle came from Jacqueline. Then it transitioned into uproarious laughter. Laughter from the spectators ceased as confusion ran rampant throughout the crowd. None of them could comprehend why in the world was Barris laughing?

The group was laughing at the vice president not with her. Jacqueline reached behind herself and pulled out a mask. She promptly pulled it over her head.

"Ha, ha, ha, ha. Never again. Release the poisonous gas!" Barris exclaimed.

To The People Of Wauconda.........

A thick misty cloud engulfed the room. People coughed and gagged on the toxic fumes. Some of them started regurgitating blood. Additional laughter erupted from Jacqueline.

"When it comes to passing this particular gas, guilty as charged," Barris said. Ha, ha, ha, ha, ha, ha. Whew, Somebody better crack open a window. Ha, ha, ha, ha, ha, ha. Your very lives depend on it," she said.

Triden watched the entire sordid affair as it unfolded live on national television along with some of his administarative staff members. Bo stood behind his desk in disbelief. His Secretarty Of State, Tony Dinky cried out.

"For God's sake, you've got to do something! She's your vice president!" Dinky exclaimed.

Triden began to mutter, "Ba, blah, ba. Beans a quarter of ham. Sis boom bah, Ricky icky. Ah, ah... We beat Medicare!" Bo shouted.

The president appeared to be more confused than ever. A few minutes later, Bo managed to come to his senses and began to speak while using a rational train of thought.

"Send an extraction team to recover Barris also any and all evidence. Bring Jacqueline here to safety. No matter what the American people have seen today, it never happened. None of it. We will deny all accountability. Deny, deny," Bo said.

Put Him Out To Pasteur

By popular consensus "Bizarre" became the word of choice to describe this presidency. A family from West Virginia won free passes to visit the White House and meet the president. This particular unit of kinfolk consisted of a married couple and their six year old daughter. After touring the White House they were led into the Oval Office which is where the president greeted them. Instead of shaking hands with the man and woman, Triden got down on one knee and held their daughter close.

He sniffed the girl's hair several times before releasing a sigh of satisfaction. Bo told the girl that her hair smelled "April fresh" and he was crazy about her. An awkward moment for the parents, as they grabbed their daughter and fled the White House with haste. The president felt giddy.

He scratched his crotch and smiled with anticipation for the day that was ahead. There was also a stark raving lunatic that held the title of Vice President. Together there isn't anything that these two can do right. Bo Triden decided to reunite with his old barbershop quartet. Their group is aptly named, Extremely Confused.

They had a brand new song. The president wrote it himself. His intention was for the group to perform it live on national television with full media coverage. On the day of the performance the barbershop quartet arrived at the studio right on time. All four gentlemen were coordinated and dressed for the occasion. They were all wearing matching outfits.

The suits were well fitted.Their attire also included hats. The time had come to go live and the cameras were rolling.

Extremely Confused Perform Live!

Put Him Out
To Pasteur-The Song

♪Doo Wop, Doo Wop, Doo, Wop♪

♪I met a girl named Marion walking down♪

♪Sunset Boulevard♪

♪Didn't allow her to get far/ Said,♪

♪"Bitch, get in the car"♪

♪Rest assure, I didn't have to use any dirty tricks♪

♪She was already out there on the♪

♪street turning tricks♪

♪This girl got me so infatuated♪

♪it really made me sick♪

♪Got quite a surprise when♪

♪Marion pulled up her dress/♪

♪She had a big ol' dick♪

♪What is a woman?/♪

♪It can be anything that you like♪

♪Put my thing up in her butt and♪

♪it was a delight♪

♪ - Shimity boo bop, Shimity boo, ♪
♪ Shimity boo bop, Shimity boo - ♪
♪ Shimity boo bop, Shimity boo, ♪
♪ Shimity boo bop, Shimity boo, ♪
♪ what'll you do? ♪
♪ During the mid 80s ♪
♪ I was out on the West Coast ♪
♪ Truly in dire need of what I crave most ♪
♪ Extremely drunk and confident ♪
♪ that it was in range ♪
♪ No way in Hell I'm going home ♪
♪ without finding some "strange" ♪
♪ Walked by a lady in the alley/ ♪
♪ She appeared to be second rate ♪
♪ She asked, "Hey honey, ♪
♪ are you looking for a date?" ♪
♪ Didn't have much time to spare ♪
♪ it was getting late ♪
♪ Told her, "I have fifteen dollars/ ♪
♪ Take it or leave it/ ♪

♪Don't want to negotiate" ♪

♪-Shimity boo bop, Shimity boo, ♪

♪Shimity boo bop, Shimity boo - ♪

♪Shimity boo bop, Shimity boo, ♪

♪Shimity boo bop, Shimity boo, ♪

♪what'll you do? ♪

♪Never free based crack before/ ♪

♪I prefer it in the powder form ♪

♪Busy looking for some toot/ ♪

♪Don't play the bugle or a horn ♪

♪Found some then used a credit ♪

♪card to line up some blow ♪

♪It wasn't Christmas but there ♪

♪was a blizzard worth of snow ♪

♪My lady was feeling down so she took a hit ♪

♪Then she made me laugh/ What is it, ♪

♪Babs?/ The crabs were making her itch ♪

♪What is a woman?/ It can be anything that you like ♪

♪These days it's a mystery and that can be a fright ♪

♪-Shimity boo bop, Shimity boo, ♪

♪*Shimity boo bop, Shimity boo*♪
♪*-Shimity boo bop, Shimity boo,*♪
♪ *Shimity boo bop, Shimity boo, what'll you do?*♪

Only a couple of onlookers that were present in the studio applauded, as the rest of the spectators were frozen in awe. There weren't any words to express the absurdity of what they had observed on that day. Bo Triden started doing a little dance routine with his cane. The rest of the barbershop quartet began to to disband and were homeward bound. Simply put, this is merely additional concrete evidence for the court of public opinion, proving in dubitably that the Commander in Chief has truly lost his marbles.

A Heartbeat Away From The Presidency

It is Thursday afternoon. The president left D.C. to give a speech in his home town of Scranton. Jacqueline Barris' most heartfelt desire is to become potus. The V.P craved the role so much she could smell it. Jacqueline snuck into the Oval Office, and closed the door behind herself. She turned on the president's radio before climbing on top of the desk.

Jacqueline started twerking to her questionable choice in music. Some of Triden's administrative staff entered the office, and witnessed Barris' insipid little display while her back was turned. As soon as Jacqueline realized people had entered the room she lost balance, and fell off of the president's desk. After getting up from the floor, Barris was kindly escorted back to her own office.

However, when the cats are away the mice will play. Jacqueline became bored. Before engaging in any shenanigans, she decided to call a well known black actress, Haji B. Dempson.

Haji answered the phone. "Hello Madam VP, I'm really worried about our human rights. We're not going to have the right to choose," Haji said.

Jacqueline laughed, "Don't worry about it, girl. You know I'm out here in these streets..." Jacqueline trailed off. Her assistant knocked on the door before entering the office.

"Give me a moment, Haji," Jacqueline said.

Then she instructed the assistant to pick up her dry cleaning, order lunch, set up a hair appointment, reschedule one of her meetings, have her car washed, bring in copies of both the reports and transcript from N.A.T.O., switch her pilates instructor back to Dina, and to bring her a large hazelnut cappuccino with extra foam. Barris' assistant left the office in a hurry after receiving the VP's orders.

Jacqueline continued on with her phone call. "As I was saying, girl. I'm struggling out here in these streets. Hustling for the American people," she said.

The absurdity of this phone call persisted for an additional ten minutes. Afterward, the Vice President stood up from her desk. The time had come for the entire world to learn just how ambitious, dedicated, and utterly insane Jacqueline Barris really is. She grabbed a few things from out of her desk, then proceeded in climbing out of the window. None of the inept secret service men or security witnessed her leaving the grounds of the White House.

Over on the sidewalk a woman was pushing a carriage that contained her newborn infant. Jacqueline was walking in the opposite direction. As soon as Barris was in range she kicked the baby stroller into the street. An oncoming ice cream truck that was moving at the full speed limit ran over the stroller only moments later. The truck flipped onto its side, and crashed into some cars that were parked nearby.

The mother bellowed while running into the street, and discovering her flattened infant submerged in a pool of melted butterscotch ice cream. The vice president had a look of astonishment spread across her face.

"It seems that "catastrophe" is the flavor of the day," Jacqueline said. "Ha, ha, ha, ha, ha, ha!"

Barris took off running in a completely different direction. Finally after a few blocks she stopped in front of a pawn shop.

Jacqueline entered the establishment and wished to speak with the owner. The vice president was interested in purchasing a nine millimeter Glock Handgun.

The owner was more than happy to sell her a firearm but insisted in Barris filling out some paperwork first. This request angered Jacqueline immensely.

"I am the Vice President Of The United States Of America. You will allow me access behind your counter to acquire any and all necessary artillery. If you do not, I will return with a group of C.I.A. operatives that will personally escort you to Guantanamo Bay. You'll be in there so long you'll forget what color is the sun. Now may I go back there?" Jacqueline asked.

Sweat began to trickle down the shopowner's forehead.

Twerking At The White House

"Of course you can," he replied.

Then the proprietor granted Barris admittance to the back area. The vice president now had access to all of the artillery that was located behind the counter. Jacqueline became impatient and shoved the store owner out of the way. She grabbed a bag and loaded it with weapons and large quanities of ammunition. Before leaving, Barris smiled at the shopkeeper, and politely waved good bye.

Then she cocked her gun and lodged a bullet directly into his face. That glock came in handy after all. Some time after leaving the shop Jacqueline came across a park that was contiguous with Jensen Pond. An elderly man stood up from the bench that he had been sitting on for so long, and started feeding bread to the flock of pigeons that surrounded him. Jacqueline became furious at this sight.

"Damn this old peckerhead. People like this are one of the reasons why I had to have my car washed today. Causing it to be covered with copious amounts of bird shit," Barris thought.

Madam Vice President reached inside of the bag and pulled out

A stick of dynamite. After lighting the fuse with a cigarette lighter, she crept up behind her unsuspecting victim and placed the explosive underneath the bench. Then Jacqueline skipped merrily out of the park. When the dynamite exploded large bloody chunks of the senior citizen and feathers filled the air.

Eight minutes passed since the explosion. Jacqueline made her way to Aders Street. A young female, Right Wing Extremist was talking in a large open area with freshly mowed grass. She stood on a platform using a podium to spew Right Wing propaganda and many outlandish conspiracy theories targeting "The Left". Jacqueline heard enough of this babble.

The vice president ran toward the stage. Then she pulled an axe out of her bag. The Right Wing speaker screamed and leapt down onto the ground. Before she could move any further, Barris flung the axe. It hit the young woman directly in the back of her head.

She fell to the ground with the blade lodged in her skull.

Jacqueline smiled. "Now that's what I call using your head," she said. "Ha, ha, ha, ha, ha, ha!"

Then she reached inside of the bag and pulled out an AK-47 Russian assault rifle. People screamed and they started to run. Barris dropped the bag and fired warning shots into the air. She ordered the large crowd not to disperse and gather closer around the platform. The vice president climbed on top of the stage and stood before the podium.

Barris truly had an opportunity to spread a message of love and unity and to prove her competence at the job. She could've given a demonstration of why people should be eager to see Jacqueline sitting in the Oval Office one day. Instead of all this she chose to sing a song.

A Heartbeat Away From The Presidency - The Song

♪Trying to think of what to say next as♪

♪I prepare word salads♪

♪I'm keeping my mouth wide♪

♪open to receive a phallus♪

♪Willie told me that his political♪

♪influence is all that I need♪

♪Breathe through your nose♪

♪while your down on your knees♪

♪Lock the gates/ let loose the hounds/♪

♪they won't get far/ sound the alarm♪

♪My harshest critics from conservative♪

♪news outlets are on pace to face bodily harm♪

♪I want your applause/ Why don't you clap?/♪

♪STDs/ I have the clap♪

♪I'm the type of woman that put♪

♪Walk In clinics on the map♪

Rodeo, Rodeo, Rodeo, Rodeo

If you dare to cross me

you will reap what you sow

You'll learn to love my infectious laugh

Potus' policies I'm afraid that

I don't know half

I'm a ticking time bomb and

I know we'll have a blast

Raise a glass for the cause/

I will gladly make a toast

You all think of me as comedy relief/

I'm the one you want to roast

They call me Cackling Jacqueline/

The Democratic Hyena

If you dare to come here/

Step into the arena

Didn't hear it from me,

but the president's cognitive

state is precarious

If his wife takes a nasty spill

♪down the stairs that'll be hilarious♪

♪The shrew told me to go fuck myself♪

♪during a phone call from out of state♪

♪Because I kicked her husband's ass♪

♪during the democratic Primary debates♪

♪Rodeo, Rodeo, Rodeo, Rodeo,♪

♪Contrary to Triden's son♪

♪I'm high on life not on blow♪

♪You'll learn to love my infectious laugh♪

♪Potus' policies/ I'm afraid I don't know half♪

♪Here I'll be speaking on the president's behalf♪

♪I'm a ticking time bomb and♪

♪I know we'll have a blast♪

♪Ha, ha, ha/ Can't help but grin/♪

♪I can be unburdened by what has been♪

♪Speaking incoherent gibberish as a clucking hen♪

♪The president's wife is a callous cunt♪

♪with an extremely short fuse♪

♪There isn't any caring nor undying love/♪

♪She's guilty of elder abuse♪

♪Too bad this isn't water under the bridge/♪

♪I beg and beseech♪

♪You evil bitch to let Bo breathe/♪

♪You have him on a tight leash♪

♪My intention is to do something diabolical/♪

♪Out of her I will get a rise♪

♪Defecate in a box/ Send it with a letter to Camille/♪

♪It'll be notarized♪

♪Rodeo, Rodeo, Rodeo, Rodeo♪

♪If you dare to cross me you will reap what you sow♪

♪You'll learn to love my infectious laugh♪

♪Potus' policies/ I'm afraid that I don't know half♪

♪Here I'll be speaking on the president's behalf♪

♪I'm a ticking <u>time</u> bomb and♪

♪I know <u>we'll</u> have a blast♪

♪"Ha, ha, ha, ha, ha, ha!"♪

♪Jacqueline could not refrain from♪

♪laughing hysterically.♪

From behind, Jacqueline was yanked off of the stage. The assault weapon fell from her hands. Members of the secret service had arrived. Four men restrained the vice president, and placed her in a strait jacket. The threat of Jacqueline Barris has been neutralized for the time being.

She was immediately escorted back to the White House without further incident.

Interview Gone Awry

Two days have passed since the debate between Incumbent President Bo Triden and former President Ronald Dump. Renowned reporter Jorge Stepinpoop was prepared to give the first sit down interview with President Triden since his abysmal debate performance. Bo walked into the studio, but before acknowledging Jorge, Triden felt inclined to greet deceased Presidents, Abraham Lincoln and George Washington. Bo shook hands with both of his imaginary friends before sitting down to speak with Stepinpoop. The reporter asked a couple of questions without receiving a response.

President Triden had been easily distracted by the bright fluorescent lights that were stationed above him. Bo thought hc had been abducted by aliens and was now aboard a flying saucer. Jorge appeared to have green slippery skin, enormous black eyes, and two thin antennas protruding from his head. Dementia was rearing its ugly head at a time that couldn't be more inconvenient. Triden did not want to appear racist, so he refused to acknowledge the green skin color of the interviewer.

Bo's hallucinations were severe and frequent. His behavior continued to be erratic on a regular basis. The Commander In Chief abrubtly made a demand for Stepinpoop to play a game of Rock, Paper, Scissors with him. After Jorge agreed to do so the President smiled feverishly while engaged in what he considered to be "mortal combat".

All of this occurred live on national television.

Bo tired himself out after a fierce four minute battle. The interview quickly resumed. Jorge asked the president about the type of message that he wanted to send, targeting his detractors and the American people as a whole.

Triden didn't have a response. Not at all.

Instead, President Triden commented on how the Taliban completely took over after withdrawing U.S Troops from Afghanistan.

He simply shrugged his shoulders. "I guess that twenty year war was for nothing," he said.

Jorge decided to address the high rate at which illegal immigrants are entering the country, and a large portion of them are automatically receiving green cards.

The president smiled. "Well of course illegal immigrants are welcome. The more the merrier. How else will I get the votes required to win this election?" Triden asked.

The president went on to complain about the convenience of having a long hanging scrotum. Then he claimed to be an Indian. Promptly standing up from his chair, he began to ululate and chant while dancing around his make- believe tepee. Jorge pleaded with the president to be seated and continue on with the interview.

When Triden sat down, both men heard a "splat". The appearance of melancholy spread across Bo's face like a wild fire.

"Uh oh, I think I pooped my pants," The president said. "Camille, come change my diaper! Papa's got a brand new bag!" Bo exclaimed.

And just like that the interview was over.

The President Shaking Hands With Imaginary Friends

Call For Resignation

If it wasn't public knowledge before, it certainly is now. Bo Triden's cognitive deterioration has become quite extensive. The president has become a world wide laughing stock. Donors were beginning to pull their support. Members of Triden's own political party were insisting that Bo should cease his candidacy for re- election.

Jacqueline was in bed. In a deep sleep from a heavy dosage of medication. Then she awakened suddenly. The vice president could feel a shift in the force. Meanwhile, Bo Triden felt rather upset.

Hardly anyone believed that he was still capable of executing the duties of commander in chief. Calls for Triden's resignation came pouring in from members of the Senate, House Of Representatives, and various other government officials. The day had been tolling on Bo. It left him weary with dread.

Later that evening, Bo was trying desperately to remember when his birthday was. He wore a yellow party hat on top of his head but Triden was not his typical chipper self. A half hour passed before Camille instructed her husband to go upstairs and put on his pajamas. The president reluctantly did what he was told, after which the couple went to bed. They both felt restless.

Neither of them could get to sleep. Camille assured Bo that despite everything that had transpired the appropriate outcome will be awarded. Maybe it is time to step down, and allow the younger generation to take the reins. No matter what, the Tridens will prosper and prevail. All of this sentiment and good will was lost on Bo.

The only thing he could ponder is going for a ride in the helicopter tomorrow. Triden knew that if he would ascend high enough in the sky, when looking down all of the people appear to be the size of ants. Such a wonderful thought for Bo. Camille loudly clapped her hands in front of her husband's face.

"It's time for sex. Did you remember to take your pill?" Camille asked.

Bo turned toward Camille. "I did. But I can't remember what I do for a living," Bo replied.

Camille smiled with lust in her cold heart for her decrepit husband.

"It doesn't matter. The only thing of significance is what you do right now," she said.

Bo showcased both a blank yet confused expression. "Can I have a cookie after?" The president asked.

Camille began to disrobe. "Sure you can, Bo. Sure you can. But you have to do a good job," Camille said.

The president briefly pouted. "Oh, alright," he said.

Then Camille exposed herself to him. "Now come here Bo and give these a squeeze," Camille said. "You're gonna like 'em'."

Coming To Terms

A decision had to be made. Eventually it was determined that even Camille Triden could no longer keep up this farce. An illusion that presents Bo as a capable and rational human being that has all of his faculties. After careful consideration President Bo Triden's campaign for re- election has been suspended. This resolution is best for Triden's family, Bo himself, and most importantly the American people. Now the man can finish his term, eat some rice bean soup, and have flatulence with pride.

The President is on the Prowl

Epilogue

Deep within the shadows of the West Wing the Vice President lurks. Upon announcing his suspended re-election bid, Bo Triden endorsed Jacqueline Barris as the next President Of The United States. Maniacal laughter propelled throughout the White House. The walls vibrated down to their very core. A sinister element sent ice cold chills up the spines of White House staff members.

The cackling caused windows inside of the vice president's office to crack. The story of Jacqueline Barris has just begun.

Sean Seville is an author/entertainer
from Chicago, Illinois.

www.ingramcontent.com/pod-product-compliance
Lightning Source LLC
Chambersburg PA
CBHW081725120626
46550CB00010B/3251